HAPPY DOGS

summersdale

HAPPY DOGS

An Hachette UK Company
www.hachette.co.uk

Summersdale Publishers Ltd
Part of Octopus Publishing Group Limited
Carmelite House
50 Victoria Embankment
LONDON
EC4Y 0DZ
UK

www.summersdale.com

Printed and bound in China

ISBN: 978-1-78783-695-2

Substantial discounts on bulk quantities of Summersdale books are available to corporations, professional associations and other organizations. For details contact general enquiries: telephone: +44 (0) 1243 771107, or email: enquiries@summersdale.com.

CUTE

TO......................................

FROM..................................

THEY CALL ME A
SUB-WOOFER

delicious chimkin

Best. Dream. Ever.

GOOD VIBES

Doing me a puppy-downy. Much happy. So perspective.

stonky but sweet

oh gosh   straight to thighs   don't judge

CUTE

Hey! I am a real dog!

Ah, nothing like
the smell of freshly
watered grass on a
summer's day...

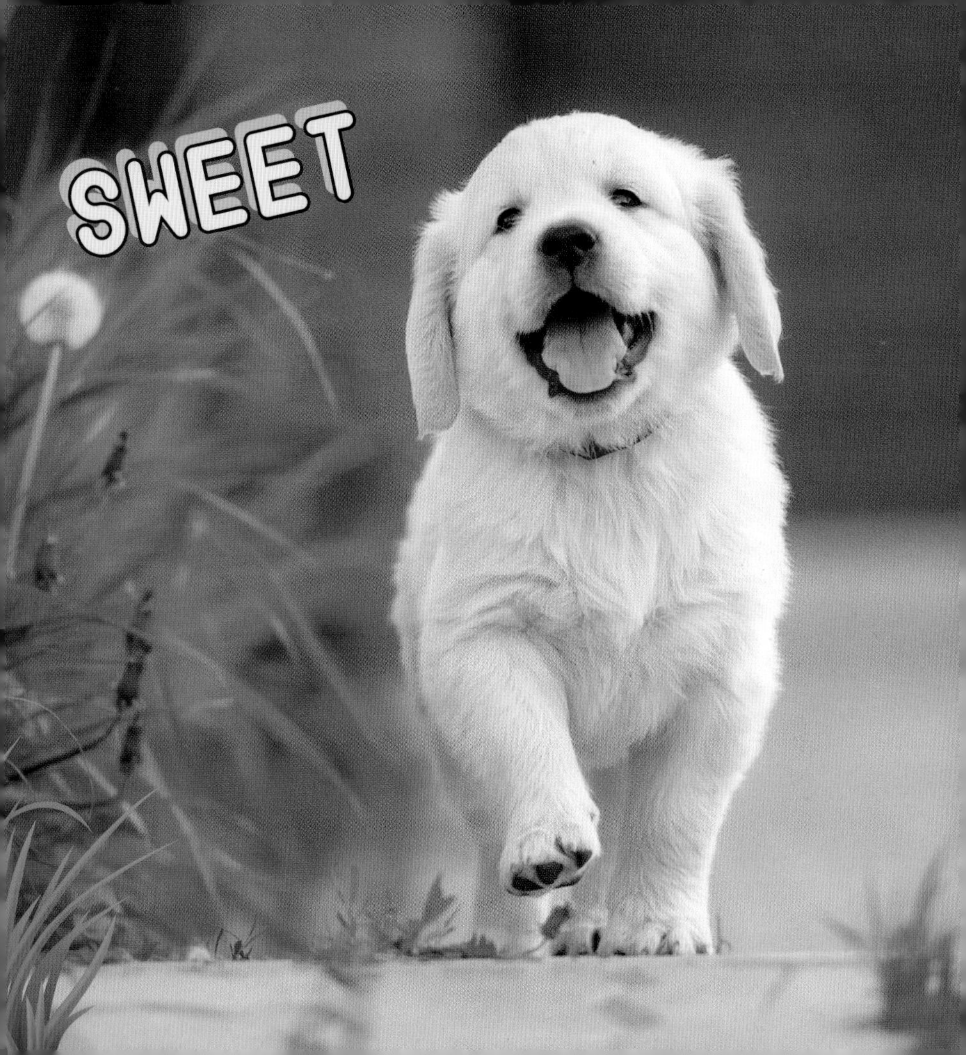
SWEET

THIS IS WHAT SUNDAYS ARE FOR.

#LazySundays

SELFIE
QUEEN

#SELFIE
#MYBESTANGLE

♥ 99

What a beach babe.

10/10
good boy

DRAMA QUEEN

ME? DRAMATIC?
I don't know
what you mean.

They're not wrinkles. They're laughter lines.

It's my party and I'll eat all my **cake** if I want to.

chonky
burrito

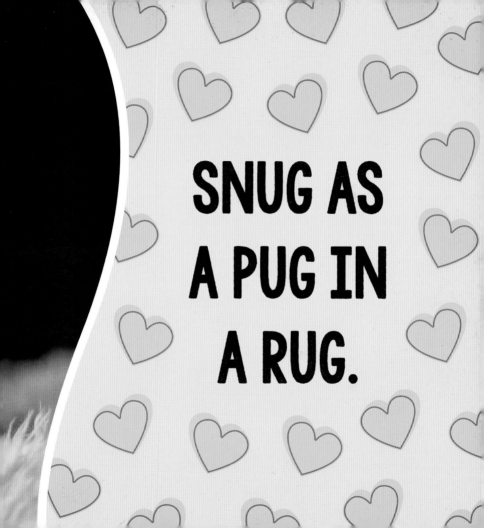

SNUG AS
A PUG IN
A RUG.

BEWARE OF THE DOG –

she's a cuddly
trip hazard.

AM READY FOR
A NOSE BOOP.

#BoopThatSnoot

**Friends who
play together,
stay together.**

Smile and the world smiles with you. Stick your tongue out and... wait, why are you laughing?

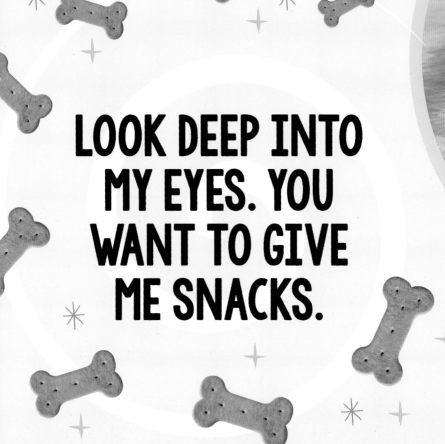

IT'S HARD WORK BEING THIS CUTE ALL THE TIME.

#RUFFLIFE

Cute travel outfit: check!

Pawsport: check!

Destination: adventure!

Tech support: I am here to delete your cookies.

TOO MUCH
DOGNIP
AGAIN.

heckin bamboozled

wow wow wow

WOW

The human is a wizard!
The stick was there
a second ago!

#MindBlown

Totally
vommed
on the
back seat

It's all
about
FLOWER
POWER.

I'm getting rich earthy tones, a note of cinnamon... and, yep, a definite bouquet of old bone.

Now you have a
reason to try out
your new mop!

OOPS!

Did I just
let one slip?
I absolutely did.

#SorryNotSorry

EXPECTATION

REALITY

IMAGE CREDITS

If you're interested in finding out more about our books, find us on Facebook at Summersdale Publishers and follow us on Twitter at @Summersdale.

www.summersdale.com